KAZUHIRO SUGIMOTO
eternal moment

KAZUHIRO SUGIMOTO

eternal moment

stichting
kunstboek

PREFACE

First of all, thank you for picking up this book.

A flower's life is fleeting. I have photographed the flowers' most beautiful moments and created this book with the hope that they will remain forever. When you cut and make use of a flower you are receiving its life. I am always thinking of how I can make flowers look their most beautiful. I believe that is my responsibility as a floral artist.

It is my greatest pleasure to show you the works that I have created.

The impression one gets from viewing a work of art is unique to each person: surprise, tension, beauty, etc.

I hope you will be able to find some meaning for yourself as you interact with the works in this book.

Kazuhiro Sugimoto

前書き

まずはじめに、この本を手に取ってくださりありがとうございます。
花の命は儚く、
その最も美しい瞬間を
永遠に残せるようにという思いを込めて写真におさめ、
本書を制作しました。

花を切り、使うことは、命をいただくということ。
花々をいかにして美しく見せることができるのか。
それがフローラルアーティストとしての責務だと思っています。

創る中で何度も悩み、生み出した作品を皆様に見ていただけることは
最大の喜びです。

作品を鑑賞することで驚きや緊張、素直に美しいなど、
受ける印象は人それぞれです。
花と向き合い、創り上げた作品達に対して
何かを感じ取っていただければ幸いです。

杉本　一洋

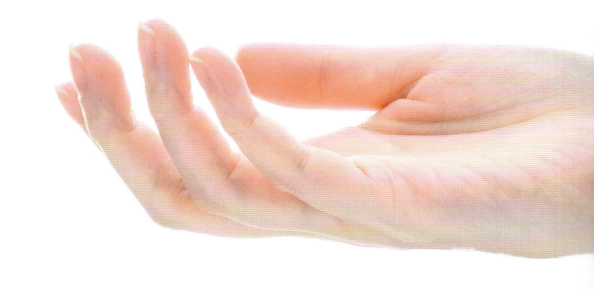

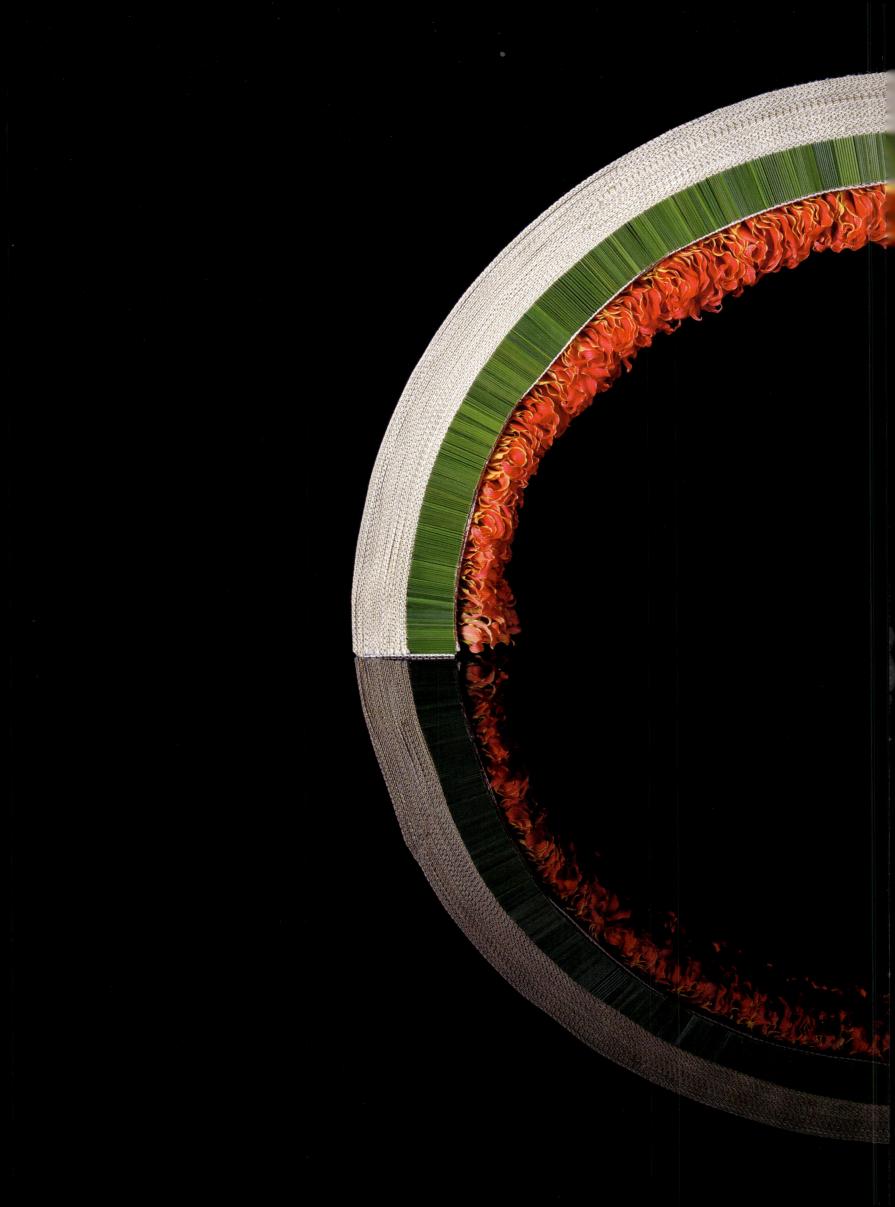

BOTANICAL
INFORMATION

PHALAENOPSIS - CALLA LILY - ANTHURIUM - RANUNCULUS - ALOCASIA

胡蝶蘭　カラー　アンスリュウム　ラナンキュラス　アロカシア

STRELITZIA (LEAF) - PAPHIOPEDILUM - VIBURNUM TINUS

ストレチアの葉　パフィオペディラム
ビバーナムティナス

HELLEBORUS - ZENMAI (JAPANESE ROYAL FERN) - ALOCASIA

クリスマスローズ　ゼンマイ　アロカシア

HELLEBORUS - ZENMAI (JAPANESE ROYAL FERN) - ALOCASIA

クリスマスローズ　ゼンマイ　アロカシア

VACCINIUM CORYMBOSUM (BLUEBERRY)

ブルーベリー

IRIS OCHROLEUCA - VANDA ORCHID - ECHINOPS RITRO (SMALL GLOBE THISTLE) - SYNGONIUM

オクラレルカ　バンダ　ルリ玉アザミ
シンゴニュウム

LAGURUS OVATUS (HARE'S TAIL GRASS) - PHALAENOPSIS - SPIREA CANTONIENSIS

ラグラス　胡蝶蘭　コデマリ

COTINUS COGGYGRIA

スモークツリー

CALLA LILY - PHALAENOPSIS - ANTHURIUM - LISIANTHUS - CLEMATIS - SCABIOSA - DAUCUS CAROTA - STEMONA

カラー　コチョウラン　アンスリュウム
トルコキキョウ　クレマチス　スカビオサ
レースフラワー　リキュウソウ

CALLA LILY - PHALAENOPSIS - ANTHURIUM - LISIANTHUS - CLEMATIS -
SCABIOSA - DAUCUS CAROTA - STEMONA

カラー　コチョウラン　アンスリュウム　トルコキキョウ　クレマチス
スカビオサ　レースフラワー　リキュウソウ

PAPHIOPEDILUM - CALLA LILY - ANTHURIUM - ALOCASIA

パフィオペディラム　カラー　アンスリュウム　アロカシア

EUCHARIS X GRANDIFLORA (EUCHARIS   PAPHIOPEDILUM, - STRELITZIA - PHALAENOP-
LILY) - PINE NEEDLES - ALOCASIA   SIS - GLORIOSA - ONCIDIUM - ANTHURIUM

ユーチャリス　松葉　アロカシア   パフィオペディラム　ストレチア
                                          コチョウラン　グロリオサ　オンシジュウム
                                          アンスリュウム

PAPHIOPEDILUM, - STRELITZIA - PHALAENOPSIS - GLORIOSA -
ONCIDIUM - ANTHURIUM

パフィオペディラム　ストレチア　コチョウラン　グロリオサ
オンシジュウム　アンスリュウム

CISSUS - SYMPHORICARPOS ALBUS

パフィオペディラム　アスパラガス　トケイソウ

CLEMATIS - CHRYSANTHEMUM

クレマチス　菊

CLEMATIS

胡蝶蘭、カラー、アンスリュウム、
ラナンキュラス、アロカシア

BELL ORCHID - SPIDER ORCHID - PAPHIOPEDILUM - AMARANTHUS -
ANTHURIUM - CALLA LILY - CLEMATIS - STEMONA - ALOCASIA ODORA

ストレチアの葉、パフィオペディラム、
ビバーナムティナス

BELL ORCHID - SPIDER ORCHID -
PAPHIOPEDILUM - AMARANTHUS -
ANTHURIUM - CALLA LILY - CLEMATIS -
STEMONA - ALOCASIA ODORA

グラマトフィラム　ブラッシア　パフィオペディラム
アマランサス　アンスリュウム
カラー　クレマチス　リキュウソウ　アロカシア

PHALAENOPSIS - CHRYSANTHEMUM (SPRAY)

胡蝶蘭　スプレーマム

SPIREA THUNBERGII - PHALAENOPSIS -
CALLA LILY - EUCHARIS X GRANDIFLORA

雪柳　コチョウラン　カラー　ユーチャ
リス

GYPSOPHILA PANICULATA

カスミソウ

ALSTROEMERIA - SOLIDAGO CANADENSIS

アルストロメリア　ソリダコ

PAPHIOPEDILUM - PHORMIUM TENAX -
PHYTOLACCA

パフィオペディラム　ニューサイラン
山葡萄

CYMBIDIUM - PHYTOLACCA -
ALOCASIA ODORA - CALLA LILY -
HELIANTHUS ANNUUS - LEUCOSPERMUM -
HYDRANGEA - AMARANTHUS

シンビジュウム　山葡萄。アロカシア　カラー
ヒマワリ　ピンクッション
紫陽花　アマランサス

CYMBIDIUM - CELOSIA CRISTATA - ROSA - CALLA LILY - ANTHURIUM -
ONCIDIUM - VIBURNUM TINUS

シンビジュウム　ケイトウ　バラ　カラー　アンスリュウム
オンシジュウム　ビバーナムティナス

PAPHIOPEDILUM - PHALAENOPSIS - ONCIDIUM - CLEMATIS -
DIANTHUS BARBATUS - ANTHURIUM

パフィオペディラム　コチョウラン　オンシジュウム　クレマチス
テマリソウ　アンスリュウム

PAPHIOPEDILUM - PHALAENOPSIS - VANDA

パフィオペディラム　胡蝶蘭　バンダ

PAPHIOPEDILUM - PHALAENOPSIS - VANDA

パフィオペディラム　胡蝶蘭　バンダ

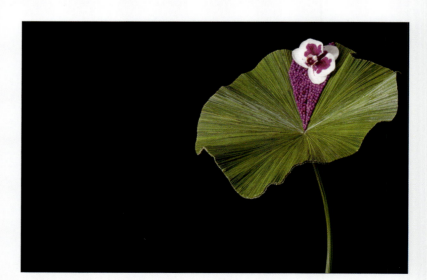

PHALAENOPSIS - XANTHORRHOEA - CALICARPA JAPONICA

胡蝶蘭　スチールグラス　紫式部

PAPHIOPEDILUM - ASPARAGUS MACOWANII - PASSIFLORA

パフィオペディラム　アスパラガス　トケイソウ

PAPHIOPEDILUM - ASPARAGUS MACOWANII - PASSIFLORA

パフィオペディラム　アスパラガス　トケイソウ

CHRYSANTHEMUM - ORCHID - STEMONA - BAMBOO

菊　蘭　リキュウソウ　竹

BRASSIA VERRUCOSA - HELIANTHUS ANNUUS

ブラッシア　ヒマワリ

ASPARAGUS MACOWANII

アスパラガス

ROSA - XANTHORRHOEA

バラ　スチールグラス

ROSA - XANTHORRHOEA

バラ　スチールグラス

PHALAENOPSIS - VIOLA - LATHYRUS ODORATUS - LEUCOCORYNE (GLORY OF THE SUN) -
BUPLEURUM ROTUNDIFOLIUM (HARE'S EAR) - IRIS OCHROLEUCA - SPIREA THUNBERGII

胡蝶蘭　パンジー　スイトピー　リュウココリーネ　ブプレウルム
オクラレルカ　雪柳

ROSA - PIERIS JAPONICA

バラ。アセビ

IRIS OCHROLEUCA - ANTHURIUM CRYSTALLINUM - ORCHID

オクラレルカ　シロシマウチワ　蘭

IRIS OCHROLEUCA - ANTHURIUM CRYSTALLINUM - ORCHID

オクラレルカ　シロシマウチワ　蘭

PAPHIOPEDILUM - CELOSIA CRISTATA

パフィオペディラム　ケイトウ

ROSA - XANTHORRHOEA - SYMPHORICARPOS ALBUS

バラ　スチールグラス　シッサスオバータ

CATTLEYA - ENKIANTHUS PERULATUS - DIANTHUS BARBATUS 'GREEN TRICK'

カトレア　ドウダンツツジ　テマリソウ

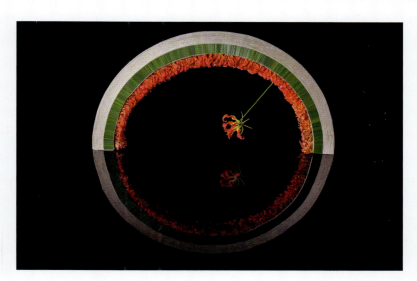

CATTLEYA - ENKIANTHUS PERULATUS - DIANTHUS BARBATUS 'GREEN TRICK'

カトレア　ドウダンツツジ　テマリソウ

GLORIOSA - XANTHORRHOEA

グロリオサ　スチールグラス

P.2　ROSA - CISSUS

　　　バラ　シッサスオバータ

P.4　　　　　CHRYSANTHEMUM - PHALAENOPSIS - STEMONA
PREFACE
前書き　　菊　胡蝶蘭　リキュウソウ

AFTERWORD

My parents had a flower shop and so I started working with them. That was the very beginning of my life as a florist. At the time, however, I wasn't much interested in flowers and was just working with no aim or plan.

Then one day, I came across a book that changed everything. It was a collection of pictures of the works of flower designer, Mieko Yoshino. I was spellbound by her vision and technique, and strongly wished to learn from her. I decided to commute to her Kyoto school to take lessons from my hometown, Okayama. I still remember my early days, working alongside other students, not knowing what was right or wrong. She taught us strictly but very enthusiastically.

As I continued my studies, and gained confidence, I decided to try my hand at floral design competitions. Although I entered numerous competitions, I kept losing. But with every loss, I learned something new.

Finally, ten years after my first competition, I won first prize in the "bridal bouquet" category of the Japan Floral Design Awards, called The Minister of Agriculture, Forestry, and Fisheries Award.

Then, at the 2019 Interflora World Cup Japan preliminary round, I won the right to participate in the main competition in Philadelphia, USA, something that had always been my dream. I only had four short moths to prepare for the competition, however, with the help of many people, I made it to the semi-finals and achieved a 9th place finish overall. Although I wish I could have done better, I am proud that I was able to participate and display my own design.

My mentor, Yoshino-*sensei* always said to me, "Take on a challenge with an open heart." Keeping these words in mind and continuing to work with sincerity, I learned to feel a sense of satisfaction in myself and also the importance of doing my best. And in the process of producing my pieces, I have striven to create the most perfect ones I can. "To do a flawless job," this is what I value most now.

When I started working with flowers twenty-five years ago, I never thought the day would come when I would publish a collection of my works. This is not the last. I will continue to create works that I can be proud of.

Finally, I would like to express my gratitude to the photographer, Toru Takeda, who spent nearly a year working with me to bring about this collection, kindly accommodating my schedule, and taking beautiful photographs of all the works.

I would be most happy if this book plants something in someone's mind that may lead to something new, just as Mieko Yoshino's book did for me.

Kazuhiro Sugimoto

後書き

私のフローリストとしての始まりは
両親の花屋を手伝い始めたことでした。
その頃はそれほど花に興味があったわけではなく、
とても軽い気持ちでした。
なんの目標もなく毎日仕事をしている中で、1冊の本に出会いました。
それはフラワーデザイナーの吉野実江子先生の作品集で、
その圧倒的な世界観と技術にすぐに魅了されました。
同時に、「この人に習いたい」と強く思うようになり、
意を決して、先生が指導する京都の教室へ岡山から通い始めました。
当時、多くの先輩たちに交じり、右も左もわからないまま
必死にレッスンを受けていたことを今でもよく覚えています。
そして、厳しくも、とても熱心に教えていただきました。
勉強を続ける中で、フラワーデザインコンテストに挑戦したいという
気持ちが芽生え始めました。
そして数多くのコンテストに出場し、負け続けました。
決して順風満帆ではなく、負ける事で多くを学び、
コンテスト挑戦から約10年でやっと
日本フラワーデザイン大賞ブライダルブーケ部門1位
農林水産大臣賞を獲得することができました。
その後、夢にまでみたInterflora World Cup日本代表選手選考会で、
本戦への出場権を勝ち取りました。
2019年アメリカのフィラデルフィアで行われた本戦では、
4ヵ月という短い期間での作品準備、資金調達は困難を極めましたが、
多くの方々の力添えもあって、
セミファイナルまで進み9位の成績を残しました。
この結果に満足したわけではありませんが、
自身のデザインを出し切ることができたのは誇りに思っています。
師である吉野先生にいつも言われることがあります。
「無心で挑みなさい」
この言葉を胸に真摯に取り組み続けることで、自分が満足でき、
やり切る事の大切さを学びました。
そして、私は多くの作品を生み出す過程で、
完璧なものを創りたいと思うようになりました。
「隙のない仕事をする」
これが今、一番大切にしていることです。
まさか、自分が作品集を出版する日が来るとは
花を始めた25年前には思いもしませんでした。
これが最後ではなく、
これからも納得のできる作品を創り続けていきます。

最後にこの作品集を出版するにあたり約1年をかけ、
私の急なスケジュールに快く対応下さり、
すべての作品を美しく撮ってくださった
カメラマン、タケダトオルさんには感謝の気持ちでいっぱいです。
かつての私自身がそうだったように、
この作品集が誰かの心に何かを残し、役にたててもらえれば
それほど嬉しい事はありません。

杉本一洋

AWARDS

2006
Second place, Bridal Bouquet and Jury's Special Award – Japan Flower Design Award

2011 and 2012
Second place, Bridal Bouquet & FDF Award – Japan Flower Design Award

2013
First place, Bridal Bouquet & Prize of Minister of Agriculture, Forestry and Fisheries – Japan Flower Design Award
Second place, Flower Dream JAL Cup

2014
Artwork designer, the cover of the monthly magazine, Florist
Jury, Florist Review 2014
Winner, International Floral Art 2014-2015
Taipei International Flower Design Award

2016
First place, Flower Dream JAL Cup
Bronze Leaf, International Floral Art 2016-2017

2017
Demonstrator, The 50th anniversary of Nippon Flower Designers' Association
First place, Bridal Bouquet & Prize of Minister of Agriculture, Forestry and Fisheries – Japan Flower Design Award

2018
First place, Flower Dream JAL Cup
Winner, Interflora World Cup 2019 Japan qualifying competition

2019
9th place Interflora World Cup 2019 Semi-finalist

2022
First place, Bridal Bouquet & Prize – Japan Flower Design Award

Many other awards received

受賞歴

2006 年
日本フラワーデザイン大賞　ブライダルブーケ部門　2 位　審査員特別賞

2011 年
日本フラワーデザイン大賞　ブライダルブーケ部門　2 位　FDF賞

2012 年
日本フラワーデザイン大賞　ブライダルブーケ部門　2 位　FDF賞

2013 年
日本フラワーデザイン大賞　ブライダルブーケ部門　1 位　農林水産大臣賞
フラワードリーム　JALカップ　2 位

2014 年
月刊フローリスト表紙アートワーク担当
フローリストレビュー2014 審査員
INTERNATIONAL FLORAL ART 2014-2015 入賞
Taipei INTERNATIONAL FLOWERDESIGN　AWARD　出場

2016 年
フラワードリーム　JALカップ　1 位
INTERNATIONAL FLORAL ART 2016-2017　BRONZE LEAF（第 3 位）

2017 年
(公社)日本フラワーデザイナー協会50周年記念事業デモンストレーター
日本フラワーデザイン大賞　ブライダルブーケ部門　1 位　農林水産大臣賞

2018 年
フラワードリームJALカップ第 1 位
インターフローラワールドカップ日本代表選考会　優勝

2019 年
インターフローラワールドカップ 2019
アメリカ　フィラデルフィア大会
セミファイナル進出　9位入賞

2022 年
日本フラワーデザイン大賞　ブライダルブーケ部門 1位

その他受賞歴多数。

AUTHOR
Kazuhiro Sugimoto

PHOTOGRAPHY
Toru Takeda

ENGLISH TRANSLATION
Takako Nishinami
Special thanks to Hiroaki Arita

FINAL EDITING
Katrien Van Moerbeke

LAY-OUT
www.groupvandamme.eu

PUBLISHED BY
Stichting Kunstboek bvba
Legeweg 165
8020 Oostkamp
Belgium
www.stichtingkunstboek.com
info@stichtingkunstboek.com

ISBN 978-90-5856-706-2
D/2023/6407/9
NUR 421

Printed in the EU